DIRT
CHEAP

HALLIE BLACK

DIRT CHEAP

THE EVOLUTION OF RENEWABLE RESOURCE MANAGEMENT

illustrated with photographs
William Morrow and Company   New York 1979

Library of Congress Cataloging in Publication Data

Black, Hallie.
Dirt cheap.

Includes index.
Summary: Surveys the past, present, and future management of renewable natural resources in the United States.
1. Renewable natural resources—United States—Juvenile literature. [1. Renewable natural resources. 2. Natural resources] I. Title.
HC103.7.B5   333   79-11353
ISBN 0-688-22184-X
ISBN 0-688-32184-4 lib. bdg.

Printed in the United States of America.
1 2 3 4 5 6 7 8 9 10

To David Freedland,
who first explained to me
the importance of conservation,
and to his great-grandson,
Matthew Freedland Black,
whose cooperation
made this book possible.

ACKNOWLEDGMENTS

The author wishes to thank the following faculty members of the Yale School of Forestry and Environmental Studies who provided information and critical comment: Dr. Garth Voigt, Dr. William Smith, Dr. Joseph Miller, Dr. Arthur O'Hayre, and Dean Charles H. W. Foster. Thanks are due also to Dr. Carl Reidel, Director of the University of Vermont's Environmental Studies Program.

The author is grateful to individuals in the Departments of Interior and Agriculture and in the Connecticut Department of Environmental Protection for making pictures available and wishes to express particular appreciation to Walter Popiel, who searched the Allegheny County archives for the photographs of Pittsburgh.

ACKNOWLEDGMENTS FOR PHOTOGRAPHS

Hallie Black, 85 bottom, 110
Henry R. Black, 85 top, 113 top
Solomon D. Butcher Collection, Nebraska State Historical Society, 52, 94
Connecticut Agricultural Experiment Station, 95 bottom
Connecticut Department of Environmental Protection, 73; Margot Callahan, 107 bottom; Greg Sharp, 119 top
Division of Photography, County of Allegheny Department of Engineering and Construction, State of Pennsylvania, 33
Documerica, United States Environmental Protection Agency, 77 top, 81 top, 120; Charles O'Rear, 80
Library of Congress, 56 top left, 56 bottom; Walker Evans, 32 bottom
Michigan Department of State Archives, 29 top
National Archives, 47 bottom, 56 top right
Charles Remington, Curator of Entomology, Peabody Museum, Yale University, 26
Rosenblum Gallery, Missoula, Montana, 100 bottom right
William H. Smith, Yale School of Forestry and Environmental Studies, 24, 69 bottom
United Nations, 29 bottom, 60, 61, 62, 63, 65, 76, 84, 101 top, 107 top, 113 bottom; R. Witlin, 112
United States Department of Agriculture, 53 top, 57; Forest Service, 32 top, 40, 47 top, 58, 72, 87, 101 bottom; Arthur Rothstein, 53 bottom; Soil Conservation Service, 42, 43, 59
United States Department of the Interior Fish and Wildlife Service, Rex Gary Schmidt, 81 bottom; National Park Service, Richard Frear, 111; M. Woodbridge Williams, 39, 95 top
Yale School of Forestry and Environmental Studies, 35, 100 bottom left; Collection of George W. Nichols (1912), 77 bottom, 100 top, 119 bottom

CONTENTS

DIRT
CHEAP

ONE

THE WEB
OF LIFE

Dirt cheap. Have you ever heard that phrase? People use it when they want to describe something that is nearly worthless and easy to get: a handful of dirt, for example.

Yet dirt, in the form of fertile soil, is one of the most valuable substances on earth. Without it there would be no food for you to eat, no trees to shade you from the sun or provide lumber for your house. Look at a picture of the Sahara Desert, and you will see how bleak the world would be without dirt. If people realized how much their lives depended on it, they would consider dirt very precious indeed.

There is a reason people don't place much value on dirt. Until recently it has been so plentiful that it has been taken for granted. In the United States especially, there seemed to be no end to the supply of fertile soil or any other resource needed for a comfortable life. The settlers who came here from other nations thought they would never run out of good farmland, clean water, fresh air, and fuels like wood or oil. They spread across the continent and cleared the trees. They used the air and water as sewers for wastes. When they had exhausted the resources or polluted the environment in one place, they started over again in another.

The land began to erode; the air and water became polluted; fuels became scarce and expensive. As early as the 1800's, a few men and women became aware that people were wasting scarce resources. They wanted to change society's wasteful habits and use resources more carefully. A forester named Gifford Pinchot coined the word *conservation* to describe the new way resources would be used.

But changing people's habits was very difficult. It took more than a new word. It took dramatic events. Floods poured down eroded hillsides. Winds blew away tons of once-fertile farmland and left deserts where no plow could be driven. Human beings sickened and died from exposure to polluted air and water.

Slowly people the world over came to realize that materials which seem so plentiful are really in limited supply. Governments began passing laws to protect these materials. The laws are designed to prevent the waste of fuels, the erosion of fertile soil, and the pollution of air and water. They should help guarantee that there will be enough of these resources for you and your children and your children's children.

These laws are part of a new way of thinking about the earth. People now see that certain materials are a very special kind of resource for two reasons. First, they are natural resources. No one has to build a factory to produce them. Trees grow and rain falls because of characteristics of the earth that came into existence long before there were human beings. Second, these materials are renewable. Natural processes can replenish the supply continuously. If you cut a tree, another can grow in its place. If you draw water from a lake, more can flow in to replenish the supply. Some processes take many years, others less than a day.

These renewing processes do not work separately. Each one affects the others. Trees cannot grow without rainfall and fertile soil, but fertile soil will not stay in place without trees and other plants to shield it from the rain. The processes are like different parts of a spider's web. If one part is disturbed, all the rest is disturbed.

In the same way, human activities that interfere with one process affect the smooth working of the others. For that reason scientists refer to all the natural processes together as "the web of life." The processes that purify the earth's air, for example, cannot do their work if people disrupt

15

the ones that renew the soil's fertility. And both processes are needed to maintain life on Earth.

Not all natural resources are renewable, although all are formed by natural processes. For example, minerals like iron are formed when a hot liquid called "magma," containing iron atoms, forces its way from the earth's molten core to the surface. It may burst through a volcano or flow into underground passages. As the magma reaches the surface, it cools. The atoms crystallize to mineral ores in the newly formed rock. Most such explosions took place about four billion years ago. The material created then can be mined for your use today, but the supply is only replenished when new magma comes up from the core.

This process happens so rarely and takes so long that supplies of minerals could not be completely replenished for billions of years. Such resources cannot be considered renewable. The word *renewable* is saved for resources whose supply can be replenished in your lifetime or the lifetimes of your children and grandchildren, about 150 years, a span of time for which people can make long-range plans. Beyond that point, no one can predict accurately how human beings will live or what resources they will need.

People cannot afford to continue wasting nonrenewable resources. In the future, for example, they will collect and recycle aluminum cans instead of throwing them away. By recycling this metal, people will be conserving the supply already available and reducing the amount they must mine from the earth.

The new way of using resources, both renewable and nonrenewable, was described best by conservationist R. Buckminster Fuller when he wrote of "spaceship earth." He compared this planet to a spaceship making a long journey through outer space. People are the astronauts, he said. They have only a limited supply of air, food, water, and fuels. They cannot take on new supplies. They can only conserve and recycle what they already have.

The natural processes that make up the web of life renew and recycle these resources for "spaceship earth." They are its life-support system. If people do not disrupt the web of life, they will preserve the opportunity of future generations to enjoy healthy, comfortable lives. Most important for that future are four resources: air, soil, water, and fuel.

TWO

THE AIR

About five billion years ago, a hot, billowing mass of swirling atoms came hurtling through outer space. No one knows exactly where it came from. Perhaps it was the debris of an exploding star. Or it might have broken off from a much larger mass. Such masses, called "nebulae," can be seen as cloudy areas in the Milky Way.

The mass of atoms whirled about. Some of the atoms collided with others and formed molecules. Two hydrogen

18

atoms joined one oxygen atom and formed water. Two oxygen atoms joined one carbon atom and formed carbon dioxide. The molecules formed clouds of gases. As the whole mass began to cool, some gases became heavy and settled toward the center, forming a hot sphere. The sphere's surface began to cool. The planet earth came into being.

Around this sphere was a mass of hot, light gases: the atmosphere. Because the earth's gravity was still weak, the lightest gases, such as hydrogen and helium, easily escaped into outer space. As the earth cooled and became dense, its gravitational pull grew stronger and it held back heavier gases like nitrogen, which now constitutes 75 percent of the atmosphere.

Within another billion years, a second change began to take place. A tiny living organism evolved. A plant, it had the ability to create food for itself by splitting carbon dioxide and water molecules. It used the carbon and hydrogen atoms as building blocks for new cells and released oxygen atoms into the atmosphere, where they began to accumulate. Oxygen reached its present level about 500,000,000 years ago and now makes up 23 percent of the atmosphere.

Gravity is now strong enough to hold this atmosphere in place, but the gases thin out rapidly as you move farther away from the earth's surface. For this reason, human life can exist in only a thin layer, twelve miles high, known as the troposphere. More than 90 percent of the atmosphere is concentrated here.

The atmosphere's gases make life possible by forming a

shield around the earth, protecting it from the sun's ultra-violet rays. Most of these rays are absorbed before they reach the troposphere by a layer of ozone gas, although enough filters through to tan you on a summer day. Ozone gas is deadly to living organisms, but life could not exist on this planet if ozone did not screen out the sun's equally deadly ultraviolet rays.

The atmosphere also moderates the earth's temperature. Its gases, especially carbon dioxide, are like the glass walls and roof of a greenhouse. They trap the sun's heat and absorb it during the day. At night, this captured heat warms the earth. Without the atmosphere's gases, the sun's heat would bounce from the earth's surface back into outer space. The earth would be like the moon, whose night temperatures drop as low as −300 degrees Fahrenheit.

The mixture of gases in the atmosphere achieved a balance millions of years ago. That balance is maintained by the natural processes that make up the web of life. As each gas is used, the processes replace it by releasing atoms now hardened into rock or dissolved in water. If this replacement did not take place continuously, the supply of some gases would be depleted and the atmosphere's mixture would change.

For example, carbon-dioxide gas, which makes up less than 1 percent of the atmosphere, is used by plants and is absorbed by the ocean, which holds fifty times the amount the atmosphere does. These losses from the atmosphere are balanced by the release of carbon-dioxide gas from the earth's surface. Some comes from eroding rock. Some is released when living organisms die and decay. When plants, especially trees, are burned, carbon-dioxide gas is created. These sources renew the atmosphere's supply, replenishing the total amount in four to eight years.

The time needed for green plants to replenish the supply of oxygen is 300 years, which is still short compared to the time needed for natural processes to renew the nitrogen supply. Most nitrogen is part of rocks and soil, from which it can be released only by special bacteria. Volcanic explosions also bring some from the earth's core. These sources work so slowly that it would take 100,000,000 years to replenish the atmosphere. Without them, however slow, most of the atmosphere's nitrogen would now be gone—dissolved back into the ocean or bound up in soil.

Thus, processes such as erosion and decay prevent gases like carbon dioxide and nitrogen from being used up by living organisms or absorbed into the earth's surface. Instead, the web of life continuously maintains the balance of gases in the atmosphere. If the web is disrupted, the balance ends and living organisms suffer.

Human beings began to alter the balance about 250,000 years ago. Visiting the earth then, you would have seen scattered clouds of smoke, a sign that prehistoric men and women had learned to control fire. No one knows how they did this. Fires often start naturally when lightning hits a tree or when volcanoes explode. Most animals have an instinctive fear of fire and run away, but some brave man or woman must have picked up a smoldering piece of wood and carried it home.

The control of fire changed people's lives. When they gathered in their caves at night, the fire provided light and heat as well as protection from predators. Burning wood filled the air with smoke and soot, gases, and particles of carbon released from the plant cells, but that annoyance was a small price to pay for the comforts of a campfire.

By 4,000 B.C. people had new uses for fire. They discovered that certain rocks contained minerals such as iron that could be melted and shaped into tools. Smelting, the technique for preparing the mineral, required very hot fires that gave off soot and smoke. Some of the melting ore also turned into a gas again. By 1,000 B.C. people were melting sand to produce glass. Both ways of manufacturing products were useful, but they added smoke, soot, and gases to the atmosphere.

Other activities affected the atmosphere. When people cleared land for farming, they exposed dirt that blew in the wind. Leather tanning added unpleasant fumes. By adding them to the atmosphere along with soot and smoke, people were creating pollution, an abnormal concentration of gases and particles in the air.

Not all pollution came from human activities. Natural processes themselves have always created some. Rocks give off mineral gases as they erode. Decaying organisms also release gases such as hydrogen sulfide, which makes rotting eggs smell so foul. Forest fires darken the air with smoke and soot. Each day 2,000 tons of stardust, the microscopic remains of exploded comets, meteors, and long-dead planets, fall to earth from outer space.

The atmosphere has always been a complex mixture of gases and particles, some of them harmful. Living organisms have natural defenses against polluted air. For example, the inside of your nostrils is lined with tiny hairs that filter out particles. The mucus produced by your nose, mouth, and windpipe helps dissolve harmful gases. These defenses protect your lungs from damage. Plant cells are protected by a waxy coating that keeps out particles and gases.

The atmosphere, too, has defenses against pollution. Gravity pulls heavy particles back to earth. Rain and snow wash the air as droplets mass around particles or gas molecules. When the droplets fall, the molecule or particle is carried to earth. There, the soil may absorb it, or plants may filter it from the air if it sticks to their leaves. It may dissolve in streams or rivers and flow into the ocean, or it may settle in the mud of coastal marshes. Plants, soil, marshes, and the ocean are "sinks," natural storage areas for pollution that is removed from the atmosphere.

The sun also removes pollution from the air. Its heat loosens the molecular bonds of particles and gases and frees the separate elements. Often they recombine to form harmless gases. The atoms and molecules that remain can then be carried to sinks by rains and gravity.

While rain, gravity, and the sun are purifying the atmosphere, wind is also at work. Wind is a product of the sun, which heats gases near the earth's surface so that they expand and rise. As they rise, they cool, become heavy, and sink again. The alternate rising and sinking creates a

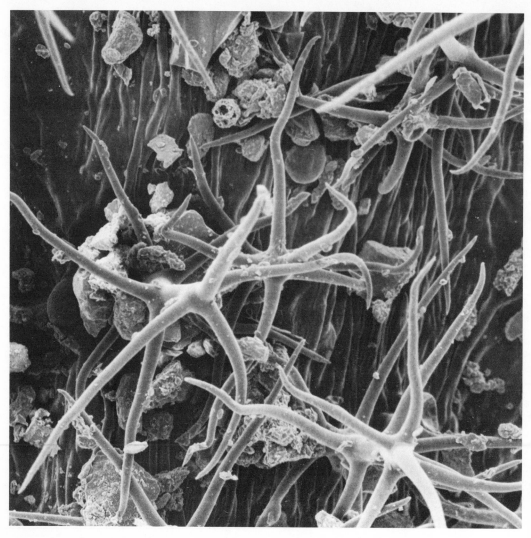

Many particles of pollution are removed from the air and trapped by cilia, tiny hairs on the upper leaf surface, shown here magnified 200 times.

circular motion in the atmosphere that you feel as wind. It scatters pollution. For instance, watch smoke rise from a fire. Dark and thick at first, it seems to disappear as it rises. This impression is an illusion. Wind has spread the smoke so thin that you cannot detect it anymore.

Wind carries atmospheric gases from one place to another. If you live in the eastern United States, the air you breathe comes from the Great Plains. If you live on the West Coast, it has blown to you from the Pacific Ocean. In some parts of Canada people breathe air that has come down from the North Pole. In other parts they breathe air that has come up from the United States.

Without these winds, gravity would hold the atmosphere still. Pollution would accumulate near its source. Instead, winds constantly churn the air and spread pollution about. Thus, to the people who create it, pollution "vanishes into thin air." The people who live farther along the path of wind suffer the consequences.

Wind, rain, sun, and gravity form the life-support system that renews the atmosphere. Normally, this system can cope with pollution from natural sources. Rarely do forest fires, decay, or erosion produce too much for natural processes to destroy or remove to sinks. One failure occurred in 1883 when Krakatoa, a long-extinct volcano in the Pacific Ocean, suddenly exploded. Its smoke and ashes were carried away by the winds and circled the globe for three years. There were so many dust particles, many less than .0001 of an inch thick, that the sun's rays could barely penetrate. The following year, 1884, was so cold that it was known as "the year without spring."

At first, pollution from human activities amounted to little. Yet gradually the number of sources increased. The life-support system was strained as early as A.D. 61 when the Roman poet Seneca complained about the smoke and

In England, coal dust from factories made the protective brown-and-white coloring of the peppered moth (lower) useless so that only a smaller, dark form (upper) survived in polluted areas.

stench of Rome. The pollution came from manufacturing, cooking and heating fires, dust from roadways, and dirt from farms. Wealthy Romans escaped by moving away to the seashore or the mountains.

Within another 1,000 years, England began to suffer. In A.D. 1157, Queen Eleanor was so bothered by smoke from wood fires that she moved her court to the country. As wood became scarce and people began to burn coal, pollution from soot and smoke grew even worse. By A.D. 1578 it was so bad that Queen Elizabeth I ordered people living and working around her London castle to burn only wood so that she could get some relief from polluted air.

The amount of pollution was further increased by the invention of the steam engine in the early 1700's. Steam from boiling water provided power to turn gears and push levers. It could be used instead of human labor to operate machines. This replacement, known as mechanization,

26

soon created the need for large coal-fired furnaces to boil huge quantities of water for manufacturers' steam engines.

Factories were built and they were grouped along rivers so that water could be piped directly into the giant boilers. These factories formed industrial centers that replaced the scattered workshops of earlier times. They created pollution on a vast new scale and concentrated it in a few areas.

People coughed and choked. Their eyes stung. Burning coal gave off sulfur dioxide that joined with water vapor in the atmosphere and formed an acid. The acid ate away brick and stone, caused paint to peel, and dissolved clothing. In the 1800's, an ancient Egyptian pillar was brought to London. It deteriorated more in 100 years there than in its previous 3,000 years in the Sahara Desert.

Living organisms were affected. Pollution even caused England's peppered moth (*Biston betularia*) to change color. The moth, normally silver-white with brown spots, hides from predators by resting on tree trunks. It is camouflaged because its silver-and-brown pattern blends with the bark. But soot and sulfur gases turned the bark a dingy brown. The light moths were conspicuous and were easily caught by predators. A few that were naturally darker escaped. Any offspring that inherited their coloring multiplied while the number of lighter moths declined. Today the original light peppered moth still survives but only where there is little pollution.

In 1769, inventors tinkered with a new use for the steam engine. They attached it to a frame with four wheels and created the world's first car. It was bulky, slow, and sooty.

But by the 1880's, inventors had refined it by developing an engine that burned gasoline instead of coal. This car was so fast and light that it eventually replaced horse-drawn vehicles. The car created new pollution and prevented people from ever escaping dirty air. Unlike the ancient Romans or Queen Eleanor, who could move to places where the air was still clean, modern people now brought pollution with them wherever they traveled.

Changes in the atmosphere became evident. By this time, a brown haze hung in the sky. Later known as smog, it was a mixture of gases and particles that even the sun could not easily break up. Instead, the sun's heat caused the mixture to thicken and recombine chemically into a harmful gas that killed plants and made people ill. The sun also converted some of the smog to ozone. There was too little to be deadly but enough to make people dizzy and sick.

The atmosphere was like a stopped-up sink. Pollution from factories, heating and cooking fires, and cars was filling it faster than natural processes could drain it. Mechanized countries were not the only ones to suffer. In India, for example, a growing population needed more fires for cooking and heating, which taxed the ability of natural processes to clean the air there.

By the 1920's there were enough automobiles to cause traffic jams, such as this crush of Sunday drivers on Detroit's Woodward Avenue (1). Today exhaust gases from the growing number of automobiles pollute whole cities, such as Chicago, shown here (2).

1

2

This pollution did not distress people then the way it does today. They considered it a sign of prosperity. It meant that factories were providing jobs. Since scientists knew very little about the harmful effects of polluted air, few people worried about it. In London, people even wrote romantic descriptions of the sooty, brown fog that enveloped the city day and night.

Then, on December 3, 1930, London newspapers carried headlines about a "killer fog" that had left sixty people dead in an industrial center in Belgium. Wild rumors spread through London. Many people believed that a plane had spread poison gas. They refused to believe an official report that blamed the deaths on smoke from factories and coal fires.

A second "killer fog" struck Donora, Pennsylvania, on October 26, 1948. By the time it ended five days later, 6,000 people had become ill and 20 had died. A team of doctors, nurses, and scientists was sent out by the United States Public Health Service to find out what had happened.

The team learned that air pollution had long been a problem in Donora, an industrial center on the Monongahela River. It had gotten worse on October 26, when a mass of cold air settled over the warm air and prevented it from rising. This situation, called an "inversion," which occurs naturally at times, stopped the circular motion that causes winds. Smoke no longer rose into the air but began billowing down to the ground. The smell of sulfur dioxide penetrated everywhere. The air got so sooty that the engines of ambulances bringing sick people to the hospital

30

stalled. The "killer fog" disappeared when a steady rain washed the air clean.

Scientists now understood the role of wind and rain in renewing and purifying the atmosphere, but they still did not known which gases were harmful or why. An important breakthrough came in 1950 when researchers in California finally discovered the link between car exhausts and the smog that shrouded Los Angeles.

The next breakthrough followed the tragedy of a "killer fog" that settled on London in 1952 and left 4,000 people dead. Like the fog that had struck Donora and Belgium, this one too occurred during an inversion. Deadly inversions showed that natural processes could no longer keep pace with pollution from human activities. The atmosphere's life-support system was being overwhelmed.

People demanded cleaner air, but providing it was a difficult goal. The number of pollution sources had been growing for thousands of years. No one could list them all, let alone control them. Within the next years, though, each country took important steps. Mechanized countries

---

Pollution from a copper smelter completely destroyed the plants in this area of Ducktown, Tennessee, during the early 1900's. None had grown back forty years later when this picture was taken (1). By the 1940's, industrial areas like this one in the Monongahela Valley of Pennsylvania (2) were blanketed in pollution from smokestacks. But pollution controls have helped clean the air as shown by these two views of Pittsburgh, Pennsylvania, one taken in 1945 (3) when coal dust filled the air, the other one taken in 1956 after it was eliminated (4). →

31

1

2

3

4

switched from coal to oil, which produces less soot. Eventually the dirt that had filled the air of London and other cities disappeared.

Mechanized countries also established research centers, where air pollution could be studied and monitored. Observatories were set up where scientists could measure even small changes in the atmosphere's mixture of gases. Private organizations like the National Tuberculosis and Respiratory Diseases Association sponsored research. They also distributed public information about the dangers of polluted air.

Some pollution sources were eliminated: communities banned open burning of wood and dead leaves. Others grew worse: housing spread out in suburbs that had no buses or trains or other public transportation. People drove everywhere in cars, the source of nearly half the air pollution in the United States. Even where public transportation was available, people preferred to use their cars.

By the 1970's, the research was uncovering important facts about air pollution. Doctors learned that it affects human health all the time, not just during inversions. Pollution hampers the respiratory system's defenses against foreign material. It forces the heart to work harder to supply oxygen to the body. This effect is a special strain on old people and children, so some states set up pollution-warning systems. On days when the air is very dirty, children are kept home from school and older people are told to stay indoors.

Botanists learned that pollution harms plants. Some

Experiments have shown the damaging effect of acid rain on plants such as the yellow birch seedling at the right. On the left is a normal seedling.

gases affect plants like a fire. They get inside the waxy coating of the leaves and destroy them. Smelting gases are particularly harmful, and the area around a smelter soon becomes a wasteland. The pollution sinks into the soil and prevents new plants from growing.

In this period, scientists also became aware of global changes in the atmosphere. An observatory on Mauna Loa, an extinct volcano in Hawaii, discovered that the carbon-dioxide gas in the air has been increasing because burning oil and coal release it faster than natural sinks can absorb it. Burning fuels also increase the amount of dust in the air. Some scientists now fear that this condition may cool the earth the way the dust from Krakatoa did. Other scientists fear that the increased carbon dioxide will heat the atmosphere and cause the polar ice caps to melt and flood the coasts.

Pollution is even affecting the rain. Sulfur dioxide and nitrogen dioxide from burning fuels combine with water vapor and form an acid. The acid mixes with water vapor causing the moisture to damage plants and kill fish in ponds and lakes when it falls as rain. The problem was first discovered in Sweden, where it is caused by pollution from Germany. It was later found in New England and New York State, where it is caused by pollution from Ohio and Pennsylvania.

Problems like acid rain have made people realize that one city or even one state cannot control pollution alone. Recognizing this fact as early as 1944, Canada and the United States signed a pact to control smelting gases that were blowing from one country to another. Within the United States, improvement came more slowly. The first Clean Air Act, passed by Congress in 1955, made controls voluntary. One area might clean up its own sources but suffer when pollution blew in from another place.

The law was rewritten in 1963 to set limits on the amount of pollution cities and industries can permit. For example, manufacturers must reduce pollution from car exhausts. But people complain that the exhaust controls make their cars run poorly; some disconnect the controls. There is no way to inspect every car and enforce this part of the law. Getting people to use public transportation instead of cars is also difficult.

Controls on industrial pollution have been more successful. Industries have been cleaning up the smoke that leaves their stacks. Often the techniques imitate natural processes of the web of life. The effect of rain is imitated by mechanical scrubbers that wash molecules of sulfur dioxide from factory smoke. Thanks to these and other controls, the levels of sulfur dioxide and nitrogen dioxide have been declining.

Further improvement won't come easily. Human activities have built up pollution levels over thousands of years. Ten thousand years would be needed for the ocean to absorb the extra carbon dioxide added to the atmosphere over the last fifty years. There will always be natural sources of pollution as well. But the stopped-up sink of the atmosphere is being unclogged. As the amount of pollution drops, natural processes are better able to do the work of draining it away.

Reducing pollution is expensive. It has been estimated that industries will spend over six billion dollars for mechanical scrubbers alone. Some people object to this expense, although the benefits in protecting human health and reducing property damage may be worth over twenty-two billion dollars a year. These people don't realize that the money is helping to repair one of their life-support systems. Clean air is a renewable resource, but human beings can no longer expect the web of life to do the job unaided.

THREE

FERTILE
SOIL

When the earth was formed five billion years ago, the first
land was a rough surface of jagged mountains. Exploding
volcanoes brought magma up from the fiery core. The
material spilled over the surface and hardened into new
layers of rocks as it cooled. Yet something happened to
that rock. Part of it has been transformed into soft, fertile
soil in which plants can grow.

The process of soil formation is slow. It begins when

38

The cone of an extinct volcano in Alaska is being weathered by wind and water into silt and sand, which mixes with organic matter to become fertile soil.

wind and rain blow against mountains and loosen boulders or when freezing rain cracks the boulders into small pieces. The pieces clatter downhill. Fragments break off. Some are dissolved in water. Others are carried along by streams whose flowing motion grinds them together. The steeper the downhill path of the water, the faster it flows and the harder it grinds the pieces. They become a fine sand. The rock that was dissolved becomes clay, which binds the sand grains together.

Wind and water weather rock into sand and clay, but this material is not yet fertile soil. The particles must be mixed with organic matter, the decayed remains of plants and animals. When a leaf falls or a field mouse dies, living

39

A road cut reveals the network of roots that helps protect the soil from erosion.

organisms such as worms and bacteria feed on it and break it into tiny fragments. This process may take days or years, depending on the size of the original material and the number of organisms working on it.

40

The decayed organic matter, called "humus," helps keep the soil moist by soaking up rainwater. As the rain seeps through, it removes the chemical elements like calcium from the humus and carries them into the soil, where they can be drawn up by the roots of growing plants. Plants pass these nutrient elements to animals. This transfer from one living organism to another is "the food chain." However, animals cannot use all the nutrients stored in the plants or flesh they eat. The excess becomes manure, a form of organic matter. It, too, decays in the soil.

Decay keeps the soil fertile, meaning "capable of nourishing growth," by recycling nutrient elements. The soil is like a temporary storehouse for the elements. But decay alone will not make soil fertile unless the humus it produces is blended with the sand and clay. This blending is done by burrowing animals, such as worms and woodchucks. As they burrow, they push humus down through the soil. Since humus tends to collect on the surface, the top layer, or topsoil, is the most fertile. The subsoil beneath has less humus and more sand or clay. Below it is the unweathered material called "bedrock."

When animals burrow, they also make openings in the soil so that it is light and fluffy. Good soil is like a sponge: half of it is empty space. The openings bring air to organisms living in the soil and hold rainwater for roots to tap. Scientists say that the best soil is like chocolate cake—light and moist.

Rain, decay, and living organisms form the web of life that produces fertile soil. Thus, fertile soil is a renewable

Raindrops (1, 2), like tiny sledgehammers, wash soil away when the natural protection is destroyed (3).

resource. However, it is a fragile one. Rain and wind can break it up and carry it away, a process known as erosion. Rain seems gentle, but it can do great damage. If you could watch it fall in slow motion, you would see some drops fall so hard they splash several feet back into the air. Each drop, like a tiny sledgehammer, loosens soil. Wind causes erosion by drying soil and blowing it away. Rain and wind can erode tons of soil in a single day.

Normally the soil is protected by the plants above it, the humus on it, and the roots in it. Plants shield soil from the sun, which would dry it, and from wind. They blunt the force of falling rain, which hits them first. Rain rarely hurts plants, since they can bend and sway. Water droplets

42

2

3

running off the leaves then fall more slowly to the humus, which gives way like a pillow and lets drops soak gently through to the spongy soil. If some soil is loosened, it is trapped and held by the underground network of roots.

As long as the plant cover remains solid, only a little soil will ever slip through. A prairie, for example, loses only about one pound of soil from each acre per year. Forests lose even less. This loss will be balanced by the new soil that is being formed. The balance will be destroyed, however, if the plant shield is removed.

Plant cover has been removed many times in the earth's past. Powerful underground eruptions have raised mountains and shunted the plants aside. Volcanos emit lava, which soon weathers to an excellent soil itself. A few million years ago, glaciers moved down from the Arctic Circle. Four times they advanced and retreated. Each time they scraped away some of the plants and soil. When the last glacier melted 10,000 years ago, it dropped a layer of gravel and rocks over what was left of the soil in the northern United States, Asia, and Europe.

These natural events prevented soil from building up undisturbed. They have reduced it to a thin layer around the earth. It is so thin that it can be compared to the skin of an orange. From the outside the orange looks thick and tough, but cut it in half and you will see that it is not. You can scrape the skin away with a fingernail.

Fertile soil is like that orange skin. From the earth's surface to the core is a distance of nearly 4,000 miles, yet only a few feet are soil. It is especially thin in climates that are very hot and dry or very cold, where plants cannot grow into an effective cover. In some places there is no soil at all, on deserts and mountain peaks, for example.

The earth is quiet now, and natural events rarely destroy the soil. Most erosion today is caused by human carelessness. Some occurs after people cut down too many trees in one area or let too many animals graze in one spot. Both actions can destroy the plant cover. Even worse is careless farming, which not only removes the natural plant cover, but uses up the humus and reduces the soil to sand and clay again.

When men and women first began farming 10,000 years ago, they did not understand that soil could be exhausted. They wanted to save themselves the work of searching for nuts, seeds, and berries to eat. They cleared land near their homes and sowed the seeds of food-bearing plants. The first yields were abundant, but each year the crops grew poorer. The storehouse of nutrients in the soil was being emptied.

Sometimes people learned by trial and error to renew the soil's fertility. In parts of Africa and Asia, communities developed a pattern called "shifting agriculture." They abandoned their fields after a few years and let the natural plant cover return and renew the soil while they cleared another site. If the new fields were far away, the whole community might move to them. Other communities learned to save human and animal manure to spread on the soil. Both are methods of soil conservation.

Some areas developed less fortunate patterns. In the

ancient Near East, people began living in permanent cities about 5,000 years ago. This area was once described as "the Fertile Crescent" or "the land of milk and honey." Despite the hot, dry climate, its thin soil supported lush grass for grazing animals and meadows of wild flowers for foraging bees. Cedar and pine forests covered the hills. But as the cities grew, people stripped the hills for lumber, plowed up the meadows for fields, and put large herds out to graze.

The land did not have a chance to rest and renew its fertility. The exposed soil dried and blew away. Over hundreds of years the land became a desert. Anyone who could moved away, but most people stayed in their homes and struggled harder to raise food in the ruined soil.

Permanent settlements also became the pattern in northern Europe about 1,500 years ago. However, farmers there were lucky; the soils were deep and rich with accumulated humus. The mild climate reduced the danger of erosion from wind or rain.

Farmers who began migrating to North America in the 1500's expected the same good conditions, but the continent's freezing winters, strong winds, and heavy rains soon began to erode the exposed soil.

One farmer who became alarmed was a man you know better as the third president of the United States, Thomas

---

Grazing by too many cattle has destroyed the plant cover and caused erosion of the gully at right (1). Careless logging at this site in Oregon brought about erosion too (2).

1

2

Jefferson. He grew up on his family's plantation, Monticello, in Virginia. He was told that the soil had been deep and rich in his grandfather's day, but now there were more and more gulleys on Monticello and his neighbors' land. The topsoil had disappeared, and the subsoil was eroding next.

When Jefferson inherited Monticello, he tried to protect the web of life that renews the soil. After he harvested a crop, he sowed a quick-growing rye to shield the exposed soil. Before the next planting, he plowed the rye into the soil to become humus. Other farmers plowed ruler-straight rows and went straight up and down hills. The rows became channels for rain and tunnels for wind. Jefferson plowed along the slopes and created horizontal terraces that slow wind and rain. He even designed a special plow for this work.

He and other Colonial leaders tried to promote these new farming methods. He hoped Monticello would set an example, but his plan did not work. Not until the great disaster of massive erosion on the prairie took place nearly 100 years later did farmers heed his advice. In the process, much of the United States nearly became a desert like the Near East. Yet out of the near-ruins came the first scientific understanding of soil conservation.

Trouble began when new settlers tried to find farmland. The best land on the East Coast was already taken by the 1800's. Land could be had in New England, but much of it was hilly and covered with trees. When the new settlers did clear the forests, they found thin soils that

48

barely covered the gravel and rocks left by melting glaciers 10,000 years earlier. And so settlers began crossing the Appalachian Mountains to the Midwest where soils were deep and rich. Soon this area, too, was crowded. Newcomers went farther west to the Great Plains.

The Great Plains were a vast prairie with no trees, only waving grass for miles on end. Glaciers had not disturbed the soil. There were no boulders to dig up and haul away. The land itself was so flat that a pioneer hymn sang of "Heaven's Tableland." Its climate was dry, but settlers saw the thick prairie grass and were sure that wheat and corn would grow as well. The first crops were so abundant that eager farmers urged friends and family still back East to follow them.

To encourage even more settlers, the United States Government offered 160 acres to any family that would farm them in return. The swap, homesteading, brought people to what is now Kansas, Oklahoma, Nebraska, Texas, Colorado, North and South Dakota, and New Mexico.

There was one disadvantage. A steady wind blew all the time, sometimes at forty miles an hour. The area of the Great Plains is saucer-shaped, 400 miles wide and 1000 miles long, with no forests or mountains to block the wind that crosses it. Homesteaders were too busy, though, to worry about the wind. They had to work very hard establishing their farms. The prairie grass had built a deep network of roots that bound the humus and soil tight. This sod was so hard to plow that farmers called their work "sod busting." Sometimes they took a year to plow only twenty-five acres. Sometimes they even had to help their oxen pull the plow.

And the weather could be very harsh. In 1885, there was a bad blizzard. Temperatures dropped below zero degrees Fahrenheit. Dry spells often lengthened into droughts. In 1892, the last year of a long drought, hordes of grasshoppers appeared. First they ate every plant that was still green. Then they ate saddles and blankets. Hundreds of discouraged farmers abandoned their homesteads, but they came back again as soon as good weather returned. During this period, cities in the East were growing. Country farms became house lots. The city dwellers depended more and more on the food grown on the prairie, which encouraged homesteaders to plow up ever more land.

Scientists began studying the Great Plains for ways to improve crops. Leave prairie grass between crop rows as protection from the winds, they advised. Protect the humus by planting quick-growing rye after harvest and plowing it into the soil before sowing the next crops. These techniques were the same as those promoted by Thomas Jefferson, but they were no more popular in the 1900's than they had been in Colonial days.

Instead, farmers flocked to hear millionaire cereal manufacturer C. W. Post, who believed that the smoke and noise of cannon could bring rain. When a dry spell began in 1910, he set off 12,000 pounds of dynamite. The idea didn't work. Meanwhile, farmers had to cope with a growing problem: winds that blew dried, exposed soil from the fields into drifts as high as twenty-five feet.

Farmers forgot their worries when the drought ended in 1914. They soon replaced their ox teams with tractors that easily plowed up thousands of acres a year. Thus, when a new drought began in 1933, more soil was exposed than ever before. On April 14, 1934, a great windstorm began. It whipped through Kansas and lifted tons of soil. Birds, suffocated by the dust, fell dead from the sky. The sun was blotted out. People thought the world was coming to an end.

Another "black blizzard," as people called the storms, struck May 10, 1934. People were blinded. By May 12, winds had carried the dust to the East Coast. It seeped into the White House and covered the desk of President Franklin D. Roosevelt. Astonished sailors found it on the decks of their ships 300 miles out in the Atlantic Ocean. It reached Europe. Some of it, like the dust of Krakatoa, even circled the globe.

Back in the Great Plains, the wind gouged out craters four to five feet deep. Children had to spend the day in bed. They wrapped wet towels around their faces so that they could breathe. Heaven's Tableland became the Dust Bowl, and farmers blamed the soil. They said it was growing old, that a poison building up in it was ruining the crops. As farmers had done for centuries, the homesteaders gave up and moved away. This time they headed for California.

But there was no longer any unclaimed land left for the displaced farmers. They found nothing but misery in refugee camps where they barely had enough to eat. They

When pioneers such as the Shores family came to Nebraska in the 1800's (1), they plowed up the tough prairie sod and even built homes with it. By the 1930's, the exposed soil was being whipped by the wind into "black blizzards" such as this one that struck Springfield, Colorado (2). The storms forced people indoors (3) and turned prairie farmland into the Dust Bowl.

had no choice but to try restoring and conserving the soil that had been ruined. The methods had already been demonstrated by Jefferson. Now someone had to convince farmers that their actions had caused the damage and that their actions could remedy it.

The person who finally did so was Hugh H. Bennett. Born on a Southern farm in 1881, he loved the outdoors and took a job mapping soils for the Department of Agriculture when he graduated from college so that he could travel. Wherever he went he saw eroded, gullied land that had once been fertile.

2

3

In 1903, a trip took him to Alabama where he met Booker T. Washington, the freed slave who had founded Tuskegee Institute to improve farming methods in the South. Huge cotton plantations there were using up the humus, ruining the soil. Washington taught Bennett the importance of restoring organic matter to the soil.

Bennett's own observations showed him the process of erosion. He watched water flow over the ground after a storm. Where the soil was exposed, the water was muddy. Where there was a plant shield, the water was clear. He realized that water could remove even deep soils one thin sheet at a time. He conducted experiments to learn how to protect the soil. By 1934, desperate farmers were ready for his advice. They turned to Congress for money to apply Bennett's methods to the damaged land.

But some congressmen didn't like the idea of spending money for soil conservation. They assumed that displaced farmers could settle farther west. They did not realize that the United States was no longer an open frontier. Also, they did not understand what erosion control was. So Bennett showed them. He tilted a table and poured water over the slanted top. It made a puddle on the floor. Then he spread a towel over the top and poured out more water. This time there were only a few drips. He explained that the plant shield is like a towel soaking up water and blocking wind that would erode the soil. He said money was needed to restore the plant shield in the Great Plains.

Finally, in 1935, a soil-conservation law was proposed, but one committee of senators still had doubts. They in-

54

vited Bennett to talk to them again. That morning he learned that a black blizzard was coming from Kansas. At the meeting he spoke slowly and kept the senators in the room. Suddenly the sky grew dark. When the dust storm had passed, the senators approved the proposed law and Congress then created the Soil Conservation Service, the first such agency in the history of the world. Hugh H. Bennett became its chief.

He sent bulldozers to scrape away the dust that buried whole farmhouses. He hired men and women to plant seeds of tough grasses that would hold the shifting dust in place and restore humus to the soil. He instructed farmers to rest their fields for a year or two between crops so that natural processes could renew their fertility. Each year more land was reclaimed. In 1939, the drought ended, and steady rains helped heal the wounds it had inflicted.

Meanwhile, President Roosevelt decided to go one step farther. He wanted to slow the wind permanently by planting strips of trees as a windbreak. At first farmers thought this idea was crazy. Trees will never grow on the prairie, they said. But he knew that trees such as black locust could send roots deep into the ground and survive droughts. Farmers agreed to try, and by 1936 there was an almost

Knowledge of soil conservation was spread by Booker T. Washington (1), who founded Tuskegee Institute in Alabama (2), and Hugh H. Bennett (3). Their work helped farmers restore land such as this homestead in South Dakota, once hidden by six-foot sand drifts (4) but reclaimed from the dust (5). →

1

3

2

4

5

Young people in the CCC (Civilian Conservation Corps), established by President Franklin D. Roosevelt, planted trees to slow the wind (1). They made a shelterbelt, an irregular screen of trees around farms and homes, from Canada to Mexico (2), but now it is being torn up for suburban developments that destroy more than two million acres of fertile soil a year (3).

continuous band of trees from Canada to the Gulf of Mexico. It was called the "shelterbelt" because of the protection it gave from the wind.

Since then, Congress has extended its fight against erosion to the cities. Farming and grazing used to be the worst causes, but construction now increases the rate of erosion 1,000 times. Because eroded soil washes into rivers and streams, Congress is controlling erosion through laws against water pollution.

2

3

Three thousand years ago the cedar forests covering the slopes of ancient Tyre, now modern Lebanon, supplied timber for King Solomon's temple in Jerusalem. Now the Lebanese, with help from the United Nations, are replanting the overgrazed, overcut slopes with thousands of carefully tended seedlings.

The methods perfected in the United States are now being borrowed by other nations. In the Near East, bare hills are being replanted and soil is being restored. This success is encouraging, but throughout the world fourteen million acres of fertile soil are still being lost each year through erosion. The web of life is still being disrupted through careless farming, overgrazing, forest clearing, and development. People in Asia and Africa must buy wheat from the United States.

In Jordan's Baq'a Valley, soil conservation methods and irrigation are winning lands like this (1) back from the desert (2). But in the Sahel, a dry region in northwest Africa, the Sahara Desert is spreading across once-fertile farmlands because of human activities (3). One cause is overgrazing, which has destroyed the fragile soil cover of grasses and shrubs (4). →

1

2

3

4

Even in the United States the lessons of the Dust Bowl are sometimes forgotten. Only one-quarter of the nation's farmland is properly managed. Few farmers let their land rest between crops or allow humus to build up in the soil. Instead, they rely on chemical fertilizers, even though they can never keep the soil moist the way organic matter does. Developers still bulldoze off the plant cover, and ranchers still put too many cattle out to graze. People have even torn out sections of the shelterbelt. The nation loses over three billion metric tons of fertile soil every year. It is washed into the ocean. And every day four square miles of good farmland is paved over by spreading development.

The earth cannot afford such losses. There is very little suitable farmland to begin with, only about ten billion acres out of a total surface area of thirty-two billion acres. Much of this ten billion acres was ruined in the past. Much is being lost now. Food for a growing population must be provided by a crippled life-support system, which is why scientists and conservationists want to protect the soil. If their advice is taken, people will be able to repair the damage of the past. If they safeguard the web of life, they will be able to preserve fertile soil for the future.

Villagers cutting firewood or clearing land for farming have turned Sumatra's once-green slopes into a wasteland.

FOUR

FRESH WATER

A thirteenth-century king, Frederick of Germany, once asked members of his court where fresh water comes from. His most learned adviser, Michael Scot, explained that salt water from the ocean flowed under the land and came up through a magic spring that changed it to pure, fresh water. This spring filled all the earth's rivers, lakes, and streams. Scot assured the king that the supply from the spring was inexhaustible.

Nothing could be farther from the truth. In relation to the earth's volume, the amount of water, both fresh and salt, is so limited that ocean explorer Jacques Yves Cousteau described it this way: If the earth were the size and shape of an egg, all the water on it would be no more than a tiny droplet at one end. Fresh water alone would be an even tinier droplet.

Scot can be excused for his mistake. Three hundred years went by before anyone could answer King Frederick's question correctly. Why? The earth's supply of fresh water is provided by a series of processes, most of them invisible to the naked eye. Those who tried to understand the processes were like people working on a giant jigsaw puzzle. Each one saw a small section, but no one knew the whole picture. One of the first to assemble all the pieces was Leonardo da Vinci, the artist and inventor, who lived from A.D. 1452 to 1519.

He described what is now called the "hydrologic cycle," but even today it is not fully understood. The cycle, named from the Greek words *hydros* for "water" and *logos* for "knowledge of," is a life-support system that renews and circulates the earth's water. It involves four separate steps: evaporation, transpiration, condensation, and precipitation. The first two processes change water from a liquid to a gas. The last two change it back to a liquid.

The ability of water to make such changes is the key to the hydrologic cycle. Water can be a solid (as in the case of ice and snow), a liquid, or a gas. The gas, water vapor, is made up of tiny droplets. You cannot see them but you can feel them on days when the air seems sticky. On such days people complain about the humidity, the amount of moisture in the air.

Water's ability to change forms easily results from its structure of connected molecules, each one formed when two hydrogen atoms join one oxygen atom. Tremendous energy is needed to break the bond among the three atoms, but the bonds joining the molecules are weaker. Heat loosens these bonds by setting the molecules in motion. The greater the heat, the swifter the motion. The sun's heat, for example, turns snow to water, then loosens the bonds still more until individual molecules are free to rise into the atmosphere as vapor. This first step is evaporation. It can take place in minutes, as you know if you've ever watched a wet sidewalk dry in the sun.

Plants can also change water from a liquid to a gas, a step known as transpiration. Plants draw moisture from the soil through their roots. Some of the molecules are broken up and used for new plant cells. The rest is released into the atmosphere through invisible holes, called "stomata," on the undersides of leaves. Transpiration accounts for the moist air you feel where there are trees.

As the evaporated or transpired vapor rises, it cools. The molecules slow down so that they are drawn back to each other again. Droplets mass and become visible as clouds. This process is condensation. You watch it when your

Plants take part in the hydrologic cycle (1) by releasing water vapor through their stomata, shown here magnified 500 times (2).

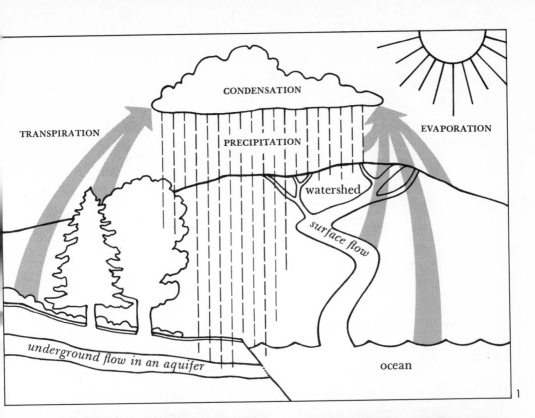

TRANSPIRATION

CONDENSATION

PRECIPITATION

EVAPORATION

watershed

surface flow

underground flow in an aquifer

ocean

1

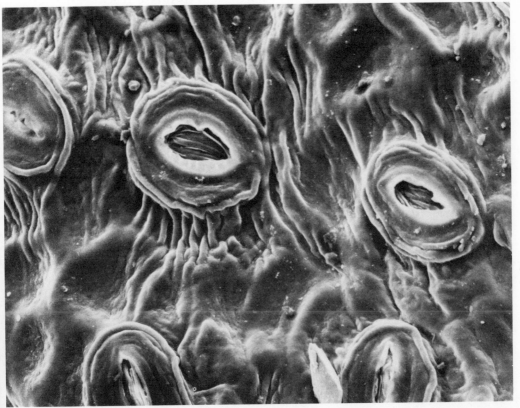

2

breath steams on a cold day. The vapor in your warm breath is condensing to a liquid as it cools. Most evaporation and condensation take place over the ocean, which is large and exposed to the sun constantly.

When water condenses, it often gathers together in droplets so large that gravity pulls them to earth. This process is precipitation, the fourth step. Once the water falls to earth, it can be evaporated or transpired again; so the cycle is a series of steps that can be pictured as a circular motion of water molecules from the earth's surface to the atmosphere and back to the surface again. The cycle began billions of years ago, when the earth cooled. It will never end as long as there are plants and sunlight.

Each time water is evaporated or transpired, it leaves behind the salt, minerals, and other substances dissolved in it. Thus, the hydrologic cycle cleans water and changes salt water to fresh water. The cycle is a natural purification system.

The amount of water moving through this system doesn't change because the amount of water vapor is constant. It is limited because there is little hydrogen gas from which to form new water molecules. Hydrogen is one of the light gases that escaped in great quantities before the earth's gravity grew strong. Sometimes a volcano brings hydrogen and water vapor up from the earth's core. This is called "juvenile" water, because it is new to the atmosphere.

The total amount of water on earth in all forms is 326 billion cubic miles. One cubic mile contains 1,101,117,-143,000 gallons of water, so the 326 billion cubic miles may seem like more than enough for human needs. However, 97 percent is salt water. About 2 percent is frozen in polar ice caps and glaciers. Less than 1 percent is water vapor. So only 55,000 cubic miles out of the original 326 billion is in the form of liquid fresh water.

This fraction is found aboveground in streams, rivers, lakes, or ponds and underground in subterranean pools and flows. They are the earth's reservoirs. Like soil, they are distributed unevenly over the earth's surface. Winds create global patterns of precipitation by moving clouds about. They bring abundant rain to some areas, like the eastern United States, and very little to others, like the Great Plains. There is a band of arid land along the equator because the sun's heat is strongest there.

The supply of water in these reservoirs is renewed by precipitation. When rain falls, it can flow along the ground or sink into it. Also, plants can draw it up and hold it awhile before releasing it slowly or transpiring it. If it flows along the ground, it joins small trickles that merge with larger streams. These streams join into great rivers. Each

---

Water melting from this glacier in Alaska's Chugach National Forest may reach the Great Plains through aquifers in thousands of years (1). Water flowing over the land is gathered together in a watershed such as this narrow, glacier-carved valley in Alaska's North Tongass National Forest (2). Small flows, such as Kent Falls in Connecticut (3), merge into larger rivers, which ultimately flow into the ocean through tidal wetlands, such as these at Bluff Point in Groton, Connecticut (4). Each year Connecticut rivers alone put sixty billion gallons of fresh water into the ocean. →

1

2

3

4

river gathers all the water that has fallen in a certain area, called a "watershed," and drains it into the ocean.

Water seeping underground also moves toward the sea. It may flow aboveground at times and even enter lakes or rivers, which it reaches through porous rock or soil. Any rock or soil through which water can move is called an "aquifer." In some regions, like the Great Plains, there is more water in aquifers than aboveground. Movement through aquifers is very slow. Water now flowing under the Great Plains melted from glaciers in Canada nearly 10,000 years ago.

These reservoirs store water only on a temporary basis. No matter where the water comes from, gravity pulls it to the ocean. In its journey, it picks up impurities like soil, decaying organic matter, and minerals, which it moves downstream. It leaves many of these elements behind as it filters through coastal marshes and carries the rest into the ocean. Coastal marshes and the ocean are sinks for water pollution. Once the water reaches the ocean, it becomes salty and will not be fit for drinking until it evaporates and reenters the hydrologic cycle.

Although people cannot change the total amount of water on earth, they have affected the percentage available as pure, fresh water. They have polluted it, wasted it, and disrupted natural processes that circulate it. For thousands of years people have used rivers, lakes, and streams as sewers. They have dumped in garbage, rubbish, human wastes, and manufacturing wastes. Disease organisms have thrived in the dirty water.

74

People dug wells to reach clean water in aquifers, but often they were connected underground to polluted water. Beginning in 312 B.C., the Romans brought clean water from the country to their city. As human populations spread, they had to bring water from as far away as France and Germany, which were still largely uninhabited.

A century ago, people began setting aside untouched watersheds for protection from human use. If necessary, they dammed wild rivers to make artificial reservoirs. Like the Romans, they piped this clean water to their cities. At the same time the unprotected reservoirs grew more and more polluted. More recently, as settlements spread closer to once-remote areas, people added disinfectants to the water to kill disease organisms that might wash in. They even developed ways to filter water through layers of sand or a special charcoal, imitating the filtering action of marshes.

But even these precautions began to fail in the 1940's, when the nature of pollution changed. During World War II, when this country was cut off from supplies of natural rubber, a tree sap, chemists learned to make it artificially from oil. Once they had perfected ways to imitate natural substances, they began to create materials from chemical combinations that do not exist in nature.

These synthetic products such as vinyl do not decay. Bacteria and other organisms have never developed ways to break such materials down. The materials even resist sunlight and weathering. They last a long time and accumulate in the environment.

Germany's Rhine River, like many throughout the world, is used as a dumping ground for garbage. The tube on the left contains dirty water taken directly from the river (1); that on the right contains water that has been purified. Treatment plants purify water by passing it through layers of sand and charcoal, which imitate the natural filtering action of coastal marshes (2), by mixing in disinfectants, and by churning it to expose the polluting particles to sun and air (3).

Few people realized this difference at first. The nation was in the midst of a war. Also, many synthetics have no odor, taste, or smell and cannot be detected in the water. But one group of synthetics, pesticides, proved so dangerous that scientists finally became concerned about the water resources. The pesticides were developed during World War II to protect soldiers fighting in swampy areas where

2

3

mosquitoes and other insects spread diseases such as malaria. Synthetics such as DDT were very effective, because the insects had no natural defenses against the new chemical combinations.

When the war ended, manufacturers wanted to sell pesticides to farmers to protect crops, but biologists wanted to test the chemicals first. There had not been time during the war, and biologists feared the synthetics might affect the web of life. However, farmers and manufacturers didn't want to wait. They insisted the chemicals would poison only insects.

Soon there was evidence the chemicals did much more. Fish died in rivers that drained poisoned cropland. Birds like pelicans and hawks, which feed on fish, seemed to be disappearing. Farmers and manufacturers said these incidents had nothing to do with pesticides, but biologists suspected that poisons sprayed on the land were washing into the water.

The signs of danger grew. In 1960, after DDT had been sprayed on farms in northern California, hundreds of birds died in a wildlife refuge downstream. In 1961, thousands of fish died in the Colorado River below Austin, Texas, when another pesticide was accidentally dumped into the water by the manufacturer.

Some of the birds and fish died quickly. More died as the poison accumulated slowly in their body. Tiny organisms, like algae, absorbed it first. Insects ate the algae next, and fish ate the insects. The chemicals were passed up the food chain. Each time a bird or fish digested poisoned food, the amount of poison in its own body increased. Eventually the amount was enough to kill the animal.

Scientists were surprised when they made this discovery. They thought the synthetics were being broken down by decay and removed from the environment. They realized that human beings were in danger. Not only might people eat poisoned food, they might drink poisoned water. By this time whole forests were being sprayed to kill insects. The chemicals could wash into natural and artificial reservoirs.

Scientists and conservation groups like the National Audubon Society tried to warn the public, but few people understood how a chemical used far away on farms and forests could harm them. Like King Frederick, they did not understand where fresh water comes from. A book was what finally made them understand the danger. It taught them about the hydrologic cycle and how poisons could flow through it.

The book began almost by accident when conservationist Olga Owens Huckins tried to stop a pesticide spraying near her home in Massachusetts. She contacted a friend, Rachel Carson, for information about the sprays. Miss Carson was in a unique position to help. A marine biologist, she worked for the United States Fish and Wildlife Service, where she was one of the first women hired as a biologist. She knew where to find the facts Mrs. Huckins wanted.

As she did the research, she became alarmed. She realized that chemicals sprayed anywhere on the land could be carried to the ocean and affect life everywhere. Later,

Poisons sprayed on fields, such as this one in California (1), are carried by surface flows into rivers and streams where they kill fish and birds (2). Rachel Carson (3), shown here with Robert Hines doing marine biological research in the Florida Keys, alerted people to this danger in her book *Silent Spring*.

in fact, DDT was found in animals living in the Arctic and Antarctic Seas. She also feared that the web of life would be permanently disrupted as more and more animals sickened and died.

She wanted to warn people, but she was ill, unable to travel or make speeches. However, she could write well and knew how to explain scientific facts in simple language. She decided to reach people through a book, and with the title *Silent Spring* it was published in 1962. An avid bird watcher, she meant her title as a warning that someday spring would come without the sound of robins or other

2

3

songbirds, since they were strongly affected by pesticides.

The book caused an outcry even though makers and users of pesticides denied Carson's facts at first. Some even said she couldn't possibly understand such matters because she was a woman. But President John F. Kennedy read the book and asked his scientific adviser, Dr. Jerome Wiesner, if it was accurate. Dr. Wiesner confirmed the points Rachel Carson had made. Although she died in 1964, she lived to see the Federal Government curb the use of poisons and find safer ways to control harmful insects.

Federal laws were passed to control water pollution. The Water Quality Act of 1965 required states to set purity standards for drinking water. Later made stronger as the Federal Water Pollution Control Act of 1972, the law outlined ways to make the nation's waters safer for fishing and swimming by 1985. It requires cities and factories to clean up waste water before dumping it into reservoirs.

The success of pollution controls can already be seen in places like Lake Erie in the Great Lakes or the Thames River in England. Once so polluted that people could not drink from them, fish in them, or bathe in them, both bodies of water were considered nearly dead. But as more factories and cities cleaned their wastes, the Thames River and Lake Erie came alive again. Now fish such as shad and trout are returning. Areas are safe for bathing again.

Sometimes there are setbacks when chemicals once considered safe prove dangerous. Such an instance happened recently when PVC, a chemical used in making vinyl plastics, was found to be a poison. The manufacturers must now remove it from their waste water and help find ways to clean up already contaminated water.

Not every nation has chosen to control water pollution this way. Germany, for example, has let industries use certain rivers as sewers. One of them is the Danube. Celebrated for its beauty in the "Blue Danube Waltz" of Johann Strauss, it is now a sewer. The Germans have put their efforts to cleaning up other rivers, such as the Rhine. However, there is now evidence that pollution from the industrial rivers is entering the aquifers.

In dry regions like India or Africa's Sahel, people have a different problem. They must use the few existing reservoirs—great rivers such as the Ganges or the Nile—for all their needs: bathing, washing, drinking, and waste disposal. The water is filled with impurities and disease organisms. People sink wells to tap clean underground pools, but they will soon empty the pools unless they use the water sparingly.

India and Africa aren't the only places that need to conserve their fresh water. In the United States, water use has doubled since 1950 and is expected to double again by the year 2000. Each family now uses an average of 60 gallons a day for drinking, bathing, cooking, and cleaning. About 700 gallons a year is used to water lawns. The lakes, rivers, and streams that are still clean cannot continue to supply this much water.

Several shortages have already affected the Southwest, where people are drawing water from aquifers faster than it can be replenished. The land is actually sinking because

In some places polluted water is the only water available. Water is so scarce in India that a water seller must fill his jugs only yards from a farmer washing his bullocks (1). The Romans added to their supply of clean, fresh water by piping it from other areas through aqueducts. This one supplied an ancient Roman settlement near the modern Haifa, Israel (2). Sometimes people set aside natural or artificial reservoirs for special protection from pollution (3).

the pores of the aquifer, once filled with water, are empty and cannot support the weight of rock and soil above them. Land for eighty miles around Houston, Texas, has been sinking several inches a year for this reason. People must pump water back into the ground to hold it up.

Rather than conserve, people in the West have tried two other ways to get water. They have damned narrow canyon rivers such as the Colorado, and they have piped water from the Pacific Northwest. But water backed up into huge artificial reservoirs evaporates quickly, and the reservoirs them-

2

PUBLIC WATER SUPPLY
NO TRESPASSING
Hunting, Trapping or Fishing
Under Penalty of the Law
New Haven Water Co.

3

selves fill up with soil carried by the river. As for the Pacific Northwest, its rivers, such as the Columbia, are big but must supply a growing population. One day there will be no surplus to send elsewhere.

Even in the Midwest and the East, where rainfall is abundant, there may be shortages because people have interfered with natural circulation systems. They have destroyed watersheds by stripping or paving over the plant cover. This practice reduces the ability of the soil or plants to hold water and transfer it gradually to reservoirs. Instead, it races over the hard surface, causing floods as it goes. Normal rainfall now causes such flooding in cities and towns that people must build storm drains to carry pure water even faster to the ocean.

Concerned about coming shortages, President Jimmy Carter called on state officials in 1978 to help create a national policy on water use. He said that pollution control must go hand in hand with conservation. One of his suggestions was that people should pay for the amount they use. Presently, people in cities like Denver, Colorado, pay nothing, although water is brought to them through very expensive systems of pipes and dammed rivers.

This suggestion is not popular. People still think of water as "dirt cheap." In fact, a tanker car of pure, fresh

The supply of fresh water can be increased by cutting trees that help hold moisture, as was done on the Fraser Experimental Forest, Colorado, shown here in an aerial view (1); but when too many trees are cut or the watershed is paved as a result of development, the soil can no longer soak up rainfall and flooding occurs (2).

86

water costs less than a truckload of topsoil. But fresh water is really a very precious substance. Even though it is renewable, the supply is limited. And that limited supply will be useless unless it is protected from pollution. The web of life once purified it, renewed it, and stored it free of charge through the hydrologic cycle. Now men and women must help.

FIVE

FUELS

The web of life could not exist without the sun, the source of energy for all the earth's life-support systems. Even without scientific understanding, ancient people recognized their dependence on the sun and worshipped it as a god. The sun is one of the few resources people appreciated more in ancient days than today.

The sun's light and heat power the hydrologic cycle, the winds, the growth of plants and animals, decay, and weathering. It is also the source of almost all the fuels available to human beings. Its energy is built into the bodies of plants and animals, is hidden underground as coal, oil, or natural gas, and exists as flowing water and blowing wind. The solar energy stored in all these forms can be put to work for you.

There are so many forms that the supply of fuels seems unlimited. However, only the sun's energy is inexhaustible. The supply of fuels depends on how much of that energy can be converted to other forms and stored for future use. Thus, fuels are a renewable, but limited, resource. There are only two sources of energy that do not come from the sun. Both are stored forms of the energy that was present in the mass of hot gases that formed the earth.

Some of this energy lies in the earth's core where temperatures may reach 6,500 degrees Fahrenheit. The heat causes water vapor in the earth's crust to steam to the surface where it can be harnessed as geothermal energy, meaning "heat from the earth." Energy is also stored in atoms. While every atom has some energy stored in its nucleus, some, such as uranium and thorium, have a great deal. These atoms, now hardened as mineral ores in the earth's surface, can be mined and placed in nuclear reactors where they are split to release their energy.

Geothermal and nuclear fuels cannot be renewed. The conditions that create them are past. While geothermal energy is plentiful in places like Iceland and California, nuclear fuels are scattered and scarce. Scientists are not sure just how much is left, but they agree it won't last more than a few decades unless reactor technology is made more efficient.

The sun's energy is renewable because it comes from countless explosions taking place every second on its surface, where temperatures are greater than 10,000 degrees Fahrenheit. Each explosion occurs when two hydrogen atoms collide and fuse, creating one helium atom. The helium atom has less energy stored in its nucleus than the hydrogen atoms. Since energy can never be destroyed, only changed in form, the amount left over from the fusion of the hydrogen atoms becomes heat and light. It radiates into outer space and a portion begins the 93,000,000-mile journey to earth.

Although some energy is lost in outer space or absorbed in the earth's atmosphere, enough has reached the earth's surface each day for billions of years to power natural processes. However, it did not power life until the emergence three billion years ago of an organism that could capture its energy.

That organism, the first plant, absorbed solar energy and used it to split carbon dioxide and water molecules. This process frees oxygen atoms, carbon atoms, and the energy that was in the original molecules. The oxygen is released to the environment; the energy is used to combine the carbon and hydrogen ino new molecules that form the plant's cells. Thus, plant cells represent a new form of solar energy.

Plants themselves become an energy source, a fuel, for animals, organisms that cannot capture solar energy directly. Some animals can use only the solar energy stored in plants. These animals, called "herbivores," store that energy in molecules that become flesh. Other animals, "carnivores," prey on the herbivores and absorb energy from the flesh. A few animals, like the human species, can absorb energy from both plants and flesh. Such animals are called "omnivores." Plants store only .01 percent of all the solar energy reaching the earth, but that amount fuels the entire food chain.

Human beings originally used only one fuel: food. Fruits, grains, vegetables, and meat gave them the energy to outrun predators, to hunt and gather food, to make tools from stone and wood, and to rear their young. It enabled their bodies to maintain a constant internal temperature of 98.6 degrees Fahrenheit. When they got wet, this internal heat gradually dried them. When the outside temperature was cold, they huddled together and shared their internal body warmth.

Then human beings put fire to work. It made their lives more comfortable and enjoyable—so long as they kept the fire going. Because the fire demanded its own fuel, people had to search for wood, dry grass, twigs, and leaves to feed it. As they used up the fuels close at hand, they had to search farther and farther from their homes.

Sometimes they found ways to stretch fuels. The Chinese developed a special pan, a wok, that cooks food quickly over small fires. The ancient Persians used wind and water as fuels whenever possible. Their spinning windmills turned huge stones that ground wheat into flour. Wheels in the flowing water of the Tigris and the Euphrates did the same. During the Middle Ages, explorers from Europe took these ideas home. Soon windmills became popular in Holland and waterwheels in England and France.

But these instances were exceptions. Most people relied heavily on wood. They used so much that they began to disrupt the web of life. When most of the trees had been cut in parts of India, people collected and burned manure instead of letting it decay into the soil. Without this organic matter to renew the humus, the soil lost its fertility. It began to erode. Much of the land became a desert where people could not grow enough to eat.

In Europe, people were more fortunate at first because there were large forests. In A.D. 900, nearly the whole continent was wooded. Within 1,000 years, cutting had reduced the forest area to less than 25 percent. Each family needed at least a ton of wood a year for heating and cooking. A small iron forge alone used eight tons a week.

As wood became scarce, it was rationed. Nobles, churches, and other powerful groups who owned the land allowed peasants to collect only what fell to the ground. English peasants could also gather whatever wood they would pull down with a long hook used to harvest wheat or a shepherd's crook. Peasants used every trick they could to reach as high as possible. People today still say "by hook or by crook" to mean they'll try anything to acomplish a goal.

People began to take better care of their forests. During the Middle Ages, forestry became a profession requiring special training, long before law or medicine. Foresters learned by trial and error to manage wood as a renewable

A windmill pumped water from a well for this pioneer family in Nebraska, and horses were used for farm work and transportation (1). Waterwheels, such as Mabry Mill, Virginia, powered flour mills and textile factories (2). Wood was cut and burned in huge mounds to form charcoal for use as a fuel in homes and factories (3).

resource. They protected the web of life by taking only mature trees or by clearing small areas, not whole hillsides. Under proper management, the forests provided a steady supply of wood.

But people forgot the importance of forest management when they began settling North America. The forests were so vast that the supply seemed inexhaustible. People cut so much that they soon re-created the conditions that had caused misery in their native lands.

94

2

3

By the 1800's, the East Coast had been cut over at least once. As fast as natural growth renewed the forests, people returned and cut again. Soon the forests were replaced by poor, scrubby trees. The exposed land eroded; floods washed the soil away. As for the loggers, they moved to the South, then to the Great Lakes area, and finally to the West Coast. Soon they were cutting in sight of the Pacific Ocean. There were no more forests ahead of them. Behind them was a trail of forest destruction.

Many people were angry and concerned about the loss of the continent's forests. They wanted Congress to protect the nation's wood resources. A ground swell of pressure began in 1864 when George Perkins Marsh, a Latin scholar, wrote *Man and Nature*. This book explained how loss of the natural plant cover had led to the ruin of ancient civilizations in the Near East, Italy, and Greece. It described the role of forests in keeping the climate humid through transpiration, in protecting the soil from erosion, and in helping to circulate water through natural reservoirs. Marsh warned that the civilization of the United States would fail, too, unless its forests were saved.

A group of scientists took up this cause. Banding together in 1873 as the American Association for the Advancement of Science, they called for professional forest management. The American Forestry Association, a group of private citizens, was formed in 1875 for the same purpose. In 1872, Nebraska proclaimed the holiday of Arbor Day for the planting of trees. It became a national holiday.

Meanwhile, the Federal Government established a Forestry Division within the Department of Agriculture to look after forests on the public lands. Finally, in 1891, Congress passed a law allowing President Benjamin Harrison to set aside public forest land for future wood reserves. By the end of his term, President Harrison had extended protection to over 13,000,000 acres.

The problem, though, was what to do next. The United States had no foresters of its own. Some European foresters tried to help but without success. In Europe, foresters are very important. Their word is law. In the United States, no one would obey the foresters' instructions about which trees to cut. People still considered wood even less than dirt cheap. To them it was free for the taking. They even cut trees on the forest reserves.

The nation needed trained foresters to bring this situation under control. A German forester, Dr. Bernard Fernow, who had tried to do the job, finally wrote in despair, "It would take a giant, or two combined." Fortunately, the United States did produce that giant, Gifford Pinchot.

Pinchot had no thought of doing this work until 1885, the year he planned to go to Yale College like his father and grandfather before him. That summer his grandfather asked, "How would you like to be a forester?" Pinchot didn't know what a forester was, but his grandfather had told him about the importance of forest protection. After graduating from Yale in 1889, Pinchot studied at European forestry schools and even persuaded his best friend, Henry S. Graves, to become a forester, too.

When he returned to the United States, he worked for

companies and families who owned forest land. He learned
to be firm with loggers, to mark trees for cutting, and to
make sure that they took only the proper trees. Under his
management, they learned to care for one area so that it
produced a steady supply of wood. Word of Pinchot's success spread. In 1898, he became chief of the Federal Government's Forestry Division.

He did become "two giants combined": one fighting
loggers who pressured Congress to abolish the forest reserves, the other training people to manage forest land
properly. He accomplished both goals with the backing of
Theodore Roosevelt, who became president in 1901. He
even provided American-trained foresters by establishing a
School of Forestry at Yale. Henry Graves became the
School's first head.

But Pinchot was not yet satisfied. One day he was thinking about the role of forests in protecting the soil and cir-
culating water when he came to the realization that all
these resources should be protected together. He called
this idea "conservation," the careful use of all natural resources. President Roosevelt liked the idea and tried to
make it a government policy.

Events worked against them. People were giving up wood
for fuels like coal and oil that changed their way of life.
Again these new fuels seemed inexhaustible. However,
people did not realize that the supply was more limited
than ever, because these fuels could not be renewed. Coal,
oil, and natural gas are the remains of forests that grew
when the dinosaurs walked the earth 500 million years ago.

98

The solar energy stored in their molecular bonds has survived, although the original plants have been compressed and changed in form.

Because of their origin, they are called "fossil fuels." New fossil fuels are forming right now. Plants accumulating on the floor of the Black Sea will eventually become oil. Trees falling into the Florida Everglades will eventually become coal. In the northern British Isles and the United States, you can find coal at an intermediate stage. Called "peat," it is a soft material with pieces of the original plants still visible.

Although these fuels are forming right now, they will not be ready for a long time. Scientists estimate that 250,000 years are neeeded to produce one ton of oil and about a billion years to produce a ton of coal. Such fuels cannot be considered renewable. When the present supply is exhausted, there will be no more for people to use.

Until recently, though, men and women did not think about fossil fuels running out. Instead, they were more interested in exciting inventions that put them to work.

They learned how to generate electricity and use the

Heavy cutting removed the nation's last virgin forests, such as this one being cut in North Colebrook, Connecticut, in the 1900's (1). The practice of forestry, established in this country by Gifford Pinchot (2), helped restore the nation's woodlands, an effort being carried on by today's foresters (3). Meanwhile, the use of scarce fossil fuels pollutes the environment as oil seeps from wells, such as this one off the Venezuelan coast (4), and hills, stripped of their plant cover for the coal underneath, erode (5). →

4

5

energy released by burning fuels. This discovery, after 1880, changed people's lives. They were relieved of the need to chop wood or haul coal to the furnace. Energy came from central generating plants far away and was brought to homes and businesses by transmission lines. Electrical appliances put this new energy source to work. If clothing got wet, it was no longer hung in the sun or laid in front of a fire; it was put into an electric clothes dryer. If the weather was hot, people no longer sat on the porch fanning themselves; they went inside, closed all the windows, and turned on an air conditioner.

Renewable fuels became old-fashioned. Waterwheels were abandoned, windmills torn down, and wood stoves hauled to the junkyard. As electricity became available, the use of fossil fuels increased to generate it. Fuel use doubled after 1950. Fuel use for transportation also doubled every year from 1940 to 1968 as people spread out from cities into suburbs. Coal and oil companies began searching for fuel deposits all over the world.

People began to believe that they could become independent of the earth's life-support systems, that electric-powered machines could replace natural processes. Some people spoke of a future when whole cities would be built under climate-controlled domes. No one would have to work; machines and robots would do everything. No one would have to walk; moving sidewalks would transport people everywhere.

Scientists and conservationists warned that there would not be enough fuel to power such a way of life. In 1960,

M. King Hubbert, a geologist who prospected for oil and coal, calculated that the whole world had less than two trillion barrels of oil left. He predicted that the supply would last only till the year 2000 because it was being used up so fast.

Few people took his warning seriously. By 1970, the United States led all other nations in fuel consumption. In one year, an average family of four used up 4,000 barrels of oil, 5 tons of coal, and 9,000 cubic feet of natural gas. To meet this demand, machines ripped the plant cover and soil off entire mountain tops to strip-mine coal. Oil wells were sunk off the coastal areas of California and Texas. When even they could not meet the demand for oil, it was imported from countries in the Middle East where over half the earth's oil deposits lie. The Arab nations there had so much that they were willing to sell it "dirt cheap."

But it was only cheap because no one was paying the full cost of using such fuels. The earth was. The web of life was being overwhelmed and destroyed as Marsh and Pinchot had predicted. Strip-mining eroded and ruined thousands of acres of fertile soil. Oil leaks polluted water and killed fish. Fumes from burning fuels polluted the air and even contaminated the hydrologic cycle. The cost of oil or coal might be only a few dollars per barrel or ton, but people now had to pay millions to repair the damage inflicted on the earth by fuel use.

This damage was documented by a new type of scientist, one who studies how the web of life functions. These new scientists called themselves "ecologists" from the Greek words *oikos* for "house" and *logos* for "knowledge of." They thought of the earth as a natural shelter, a "house" for all living organisms.

Ecologists tried to explain why the price of fuels did not represent the true cost of energy use. Ecologist Barry Commoner coined the slogan: "There's no such thing as a free lunch." The ingredients and labor for producing the lunch must be supplied and paid for by someone, even if you get it for nothing. In the same way, fuel use was cheap because people counted on the web of life to provide the raw materials and clean up the mess afterward. Economist Barbara Ward Jackson translated this idea into dollars and cents by calculating how much pollution and resource waste cost industries and government.

Still, people did not give up wasteful habits until they were forced to. In 1973, the Arab nations announced that they would no longer sell oil to the United States. When they finally agreed to sell it again, they raised the price. People were shocked. They spoke of an "energy crisis." But there was no crisis at all. The situation had been developing for 250,000 years!

Countries began altering their patterns of energy use to reduce their need for fuels. In Europe, strict guidelines were placed on the consumption of oil. In the United States, people were still reluctant to take strong action. The Government created a Department of Energy to examine the alternatives. At first the Government thought that the nation could make more use of coal and atomic power. However, the new department, with the help of

104

ecologists, began exploring the problems these alternatives would bring.

Although this country has enough coal to last for hundreds of years, ways must be found to control the pollution it creates. If it is burned directly, the problems of acid rain and smog will grow much worse. The United States could follow the example of Australia and Europe during World War II by converting coal into a synthetic, clean-burning gas, but no conversion plants have been built yet.

Atomic energy is another resource with built-in problems. An efficient reactor, called a "breeder," could conserve scarce uranium by exploding it into a new element, plutonium, which can be recycled. However, plutonium, which does not exist naturally, is the deadliest substance on earth. Its harmful radioactivity lasts over a thousand years, and no one knows how to dispose of it safely.

A safe form of atomic reaction is still in the experimental stage. Called "fusion," it re-creates the kind of reactions that occur on the surface of the sun by forcing hydrogen atoms to collide. This process produces no dangerous waste and needs only a steady supply of water molecules to split in order to to get hydrogen atoms. Recently, scientists briefly achieved the very high reactor temperatures needed to cause fusion.

Coal and atomic energy, even fusion, would create a special problem. They would be used to generate electricity, a type of conversion that wastes almost half the energy in the original fuel. This energy leaks as heat from the power plant, transmission lines, and appliances. You can feel it when you put your hand to an appliance that has been running awhile. This waste heat accumulates around buildings, creating invisible "heat islands" that alter the weather around them. If current levels of energy use continue, waste heat might alter the global climate.

Thus, the government is now interested in energy conservation. Under President Carter's prodding, Congress passed a law in 1978 to promote it. Besides, people have been conserving fuel voluntarily since 1973. They turn down thermostats and give up big, wasteful cars for more efficient ones. Industries have been especially successful at saving fuel, even though they must often do so by replacing old, wasteful machinery with efficient equipment that is much more expensive.

Fossil fuel could be conserved by burning garbage. People throw away much energy-rich organic matter—paper and vegetable peelings, for example. If this material were separated from metals and glass, it could be collected and burned in power plants. New York City and Bridgeport, Connecticut, are already developing special processing methods.

Better house designs could save fuel. In a cold climate, a greenhouse on the south side of a house would trap the sun's heat and warm the air inside. In a hot climate, a solid wall on that side would do the opposite: block out the

---

In the effort to conserve fossil fuel, a new, powerful windmill has been erected in Sandusky, Ohio (1), and fuel-efficient mopeds are replacing cars for short trips in Connecticut (2).

1

2

sun's heat to keep the air cool inside. Either way the need for artificial heating or cooling would be reduced. These ideas are not new. More than 1,200 years ago, Indians in the hot Arizona desert built a whole city, now called Montezuma's Castle, on a shady cliff ledge.

Car pools would be another form of conservation. People could also save fuel by using different vehicles for different kinds of trips: cars, buses, trains, or planes for long trips, but mopeds, scooters, and bicycles for short ones. Someone has even invented a gas-powered pogo stick that gets 500,000 hops to the gallon.

Finally, people could make greater use of renewable fuels created by the sun: wood, water, wind, and solar energy. The sun, for example, can easily be put to work heating water. A solar water heater is made of a sheet of glass atop a grid of water pipes. Below the grid is a piece of glass, metal, or plastic painted black to absorb the sun's heat and warm the water in the pipes. The heated water flows into a storage tank while a pump sends in cold water to take its place. Dozens of companies now make water heaters or do-it-yourself kits. Many handy people even improvise their own with materials from the hardware store.

The sun can also be used to generate electricity. In the 1960's, the National Aeronautics and Space Administration began to use the sun's energy to power satellites. Photovoltaic cells, made with thin slices of silicon crystals, which is the substance in sand that melts into glass, are implanted in the satellite's side. Atoms within the silicon slice react to sunlight and create an electric current.

Wood can be another source of energy. Thanks to the efforts of Marsh, Pinchot, and others, the nation now has over 162 million acres of forest reserves. Under proper management, they could supply fuel wood. Wood could even be grown in special "energy plantations." Today stands of fast-growing sycamore and poplar trees are being planted in North Carolina to be harvested for a steady supply of wood.

Wood and other plants can also be converted into methanol, or wood alcohol, a clean-burning relative of gasoline. This fuel was used in France as early as the 1800's for cooking and heating because it was easier than wood to transport to the cities. During World Wars I and II, Europeans again turned to methanol when they were cut off from Middle Eastern oil. This fuel eases the problem of waste disposal, too, by putting some forms of garbage to work. As a result, many farmers are already using their abundant organic waste to produce their own methanol.

Proper management is essential, however. In over half the world, wood is still the main fuel, and deforestation is more rapid now than at any time in history. In places like Java, once a tropical island jungle, the slopes are being cleared by villagers desperate for a few sticks of firewood. The United Nations now estimates that lack of wood will

Today many people, such as this Connecticut homeowner, are installing solar water heaters (1). Other builders imitate the passive use of solar energy developed centuries ago by the Indians who built Montezuma's Castle in Arizona (2).　　　　　→

2

In Africa, women must forage hours to gather up scarce firewood (1). In India, cow manure is made into patties and dried for fuel instead of being restored to the soil (2). The use of solar energy will help people make better use of renewable natural resources. Here a party of Russian Uzbeks, out for a day's hunting with falcons, sets up a solar water heater for an afternoon tea break (3).

become more of a crisis than a shortage of food. Only wealthy nations can afford alternative fuels.

Could the sun, through wood, wind, water, and heat, provide enough energy for the future? Here are some facts to help you judge: The strength of sunlight at high noon on the equator is equivalent to 140 one-hundred-watt bulbs all shining at once. That is how much sun falls on every square meter, an area about the size of a beach towel. In fact, the amount of solar energy absorbed

112

2

3

by your beach towel during two summer hours is enough to heat twenty-five gallons of water.

Human societies nearly put all that energy to work long ago. In 212 B.C., solar energy saved the Greek city of Syracuse, on the island of Sicily, from a Roman invasion. Archimedes, the mathematician and inventor, held up a polished metal shield to the sun and angled it so that the sun's rays were focused on the Roman navy. Within minutes, the wooden ships went up in flames. The world might have continued to develop ways of using renewable fuels but turned instead to fossil fuels and atomic energy. Now, thanks to the Arabs, people have a chance to go back and take the route they once abandoned.

Can people live comfortably without disrupting the web of life? The answer is "yes," but only if they abandon wasteful habits. The way you live in the future—your house, your car, your daily habits—will be very different from the way you have lived until now. The life-style of the past was dependent on dirt-cheap resources. That era is over.

SIX

THE TWENTY-FIRST CENTURY

It is early in the morning sometime in the twenty-first century. Even before your alarm clock rings, you become aware of a whirring noise and the sound of flowing water. The first rays of the sun have activated the pump that sends water to the solar heater on your roof. You wake, wash, dress, and have breakfast. Before you leave the kitchen, you carefully put organic wastes such as eggshells and banana peels into a special bin.

115

It is time to go to work. As you leave, you look back at your house. It is set into a hill so that the north side is buried in dirt, protecting it against the chill winds that blow from that direction. The south side has big windows and faces a courtyard ringed with shade trees. In the summer, these trees block out the sun, but in the winter they shed their leaves and let sunlight in to warm your house.

A minibus arrives to pick you up. The driver needs gas and pulls into a filling station. The fuel sold there looks like gasoline, but it isn't. The oil from which gasoline is made has been used up. This fuel is methanol, made from the organic wastes you save each day and put out once a week for a special van to pick up.

Your trip takes you through what looks like a forest, but it is really an energy plantation. Crews are at work driving huge tractor-combines, like those used to harvest wheat. The machines chip the trees into tiny pieces that are burned at a central power plant. Another crew is spreading ashes cleaned from the power plant's furnace. These ashes restore nutrients and organic matter to the soil.

You use wood at home, but you don't chop it yourself. A delivery service supplies you with wood pellets to burn in your furnace. You don't often need this extra heat. On cold days, though, you use the furnace. Sometimes you even light an old-fashioned fire in the fireplace, because the flames are so pretty to look at.

Now you are near a power plant. In front of it is a large pond covered with blue-green scum. The scum is really a colony of algae, tiny one-celled plants. They are harvested,

116

dried, and burned like wood. Waste heat from the power plant warms the pond so that the algae can grow year-round. You look at the power plant's smokestacks and see thin wisps of white smoke. The organic materials produce little pollution, but special controls remove any that does occur.

Next your drive takes you across a great bay. The bridge you use passes over the top of a tidal power plant. The tide gates are open, and water is flowing into the bay. Before it ebbs, the gates will be closed. Water will be forced to flow over the blades of huge turbines that will generate electricity as they spin.

The sun is higher in the sky, and you can see it glint off a giant solar concentrator set in an open field. It looks like a huge metal flower planted in the earth. The curving sides, resembling petals, focus the sun's rays onto a central shaft, where photovoltaic cells transform them into electricity. The disc has a special tracking device, and it swivels slowly throughout the day to follow the path of the sun across the sky.

You arrive at work. Like your home, your office building has no windows on the north side, but it has a greenhouse on the south side. The greenhouse is filled with vegetables, and it has a pond, too, with fish, which provide fresh food for the office cafeteria. You work on the top floor. From your windows you can look east where rows of windmills catch the sea breezes and west where a farmer has just plowed the fields. The furrows curve as they hug the hillside and make a pretty pattern.

Today, you have planned to meet some friends for lunch in the older part of town. Outside your building, you rent a moped for the trip, and soon you and your friends are sitting in a waterfront café. You used to come here as a child and remember how ugly it was—the beach was always littered with cans and bottles and paper. Now those materials are collected for recycling. The water is clean, too. A sewage-treatment plant not too far away processes waste water. When it has been cleaned once, it is piped into an artificially constructed salt marsh. The plants and animals cause remaining pollutants to decay or settle out of the water in this marsh just the way they do in a real one. It becomes a human-made sink for pollution. The water that comes out is clean enough to drink.

At the end of the day, you walk up to the top of your house to watch the sun set. You tell your family what life was like when you were a child: People went everywhere in cars and threw away almost as much food as they ate. As soon as something broke, it was thrown out and replaced. The air always smelled of chemicals, and sometimes your school was closed because going outside woud be dangerous to your health. You couldn't go to the beach to swim because the water was dirty.

When darkness has fallen, you all go inside. The solar pump is quiet now. It won't start again until tomorrow

---

When people keep pollution from the air and water (1) and guard resources such as the soil (2) from waste, spaceship earth's systems will function properly.

1

2

morning. The air smells sweet, and you linger for a minute, thinking about how much things have changed from your childhood.

The world is a cleaner, better place to live than ever before. On spaceship earth, all life-support systems are "go."

Earth as seen in 1972 by astronauts Eugene Cernan, Ronald Evans, and Harrison Schmitt aboard Apollo 17.

BIBLIOGRAPHY

Abelson, Philip, ed. *Energy: Use, Conservation, and Supply.* Washington, D.C.: American Association for the Advancement of Science, 1974.

Air Conservation Commission. *Air Conservation.* Washington, D.C.: American Association for the Advancement of Science, 1965.

Barnett Lincoln, ed. *The World We Live In.* New York: Time-Life Books, 1955.

Berg, Charles A. Process innovation and changes in industrial energy use. *Science,* February 10, 1978, 199:608-614.

Brink, Wellington. *Big Hugh, the Father of Soil Conservation.* New York: Macmillan Co., 1951.

Bibliography

Brooks, Paul. *The House of Life: Rachel Carson at Work.* Boston: Houghton Mifflin Co., 1972.

Brown, Norman L., and Howe, James W. Solar energy for village development. *Science,* February 10, 1978, 199:651-657.

Buckman, Harry O., and Brady, Nyle C. *Soils.* New York: Macmillan Co., 1969.

Burwell, C. C. Solar biomass energy: an overview of U.S. potential. *Science,* March 10, 1978, 199:1041-1048.

Carson, Rachel. *Silent Spring.* Boston: Houghton Mifflin Co., 1962.

Carter, Luther J. Soil erosion: the problem persists despite the billions spent on it. *Science,* April 22, 1977, 196:409-411.

Clagett, M. *Greek Science in Antiquity.* New York: Abelard-Schuman, 1955.

Corman, Rita. *Air Pollution Primer.* New York: National Tuberculosis and Respiratory Diseases Association, 1969.

Crombie, A. C. *Medieval and Early Modern Science.* New York: Doubleday & Co., Anchor Books, 1959.

Dreyer, L. E. *A History of Astronomy from Thales to Kepler.* New York: Dover Publications, 1953.

Energy Policy Project. *Exploring Energy Choices: A Preliminary Report.* New York: Ford Foundation, 1974.

Esposito, John C. *Vanishing Air: The Nader Report.* New York: Grossman Publishers, 1970.

Flanagan, Dennis, ed. *The Biosphere.* San Francisco: W. H. Freeman, 1970.

Glacken, Clarence J. *Traces on the Rhodian Shore.* Berkeley: University of California Press, 1967.

Goldenberg, J. Brazil: energy options and current outlook. *Science,* April 14, 1978, 200:158-164.

Hammond, Allen L. Photosynthetic solar energy: rediscovering biomass fuels. *Science,* August 19, 1979, 197:745-746.

Hammond, Allen L., and Metz, William D. Solar energy research: making solar after the nuclear model? *Science,* July 15, 1977, 197:241-244.

———. Capturing sunlight: a revolution in collector design. *Science,* July 7, 1978, 201:36-39.

Harte, John, and El-Gasseir, Mohamed. Energy and water. *Science,* February 10, 1978, 199:623-624.

Haskins, Charles H. *Studies in the History of Medieval Science.* Cambridge: Harvard University Press, 1924.

122

Bibliography

Howe, James W., and Knowland, William E. Transferring solar technology. *Science*, September 9, 1977, 197:1034.

Johnson, Vance. *Heaven's Tableland*. New York: Farrar, Straus & Co., 1947.

Kazmann, Raphael G. *Modern Hydrology*. New York: Harper & Row, 1965.

Kelly, Henry. Photovoltaic power systems: a tour through the alternatives. *Science*, February 10, 1978, 199:634-643.

Lave, Lester B., and Seskin, Eugene P. *Air Pollution and Human Health*. Baltimore: Johns Hopkins University Press, 1977.

Leopold, Luna B. *Water, A Primer*. San Francisco: W. H. Freeman, 1974.

McHale, John. *World Facts and Trends*. New York: Macmillan Co., Collier Books, 1972.

Marsh, George Perkins. *Man and Nature*. Cambridge: Harvard University Press, 1965.

National Academy of Science Committee on Geologic Sciences. *The Earth and Human Affairs*. New York: Harper & Row, Canfield Press, 1972.

Neugebauer, O. *The Exact Sciences in Antiquity*. Providence: Brown University Press, 1957.

Odum, Eugene P. *Fundamentals of Ecology*. Philadelphia: W. B. Saunders, 1971.

Pinchot, Gifford. *Breaking New Ground*. Seattle: University of Washington Press, 1971.

Roueche, Berton. *Eleven Blue Men, and Other Narratives of Medical Detection*. Boston: Little, Brown & Co., 1953.

Shands, William E., and Healy, Robert G., *The Lands Nobody Wanted*. Washington, D.C.: The Conservation Foundation, 1977.

Stern, Arthur C., et al. *Fundamentals of Air Pollution*. New York: Academic Press, 1973.

Steiner, Don, and Clarke, John F. The Tokamak: Model T fusion reactor. *Science*, March 31, 1978, 199:1395-1403.

Viessman, Warren, Jr., et al. *Introduction to Hydrology*. New York: Intext Education Publishers, 1972.

Wishart, Ronald S., Industrial energy in transition: a petrochemical perspective. *Science*, February 10, 1978, 199:614-618.

Wisler, C. O., and Brater, E. F. *Hydrology*. New York: John Wiley & Sons, 1967.

INDEX

*denotes illustration

124

Index